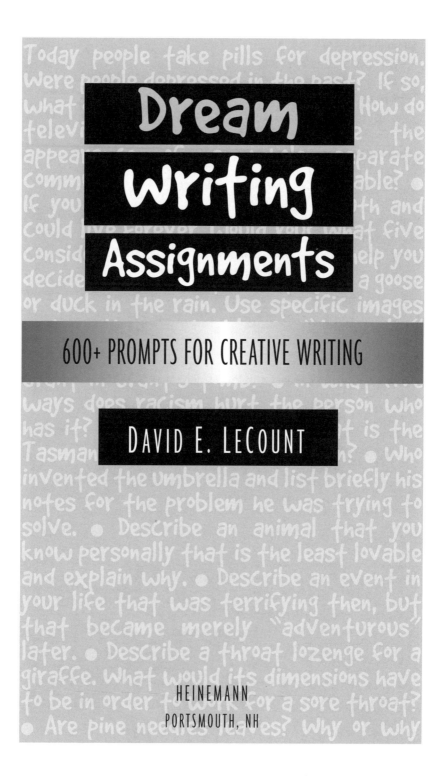

Dream Writing Assignments

600+ PROMPTS FOR CREATIVE WRITING

DAVID E. LECOUNT

HEINEMANN
PORTSMOUTH, NH

Heinemann

A division of Reed Elsevier Inc.

361 Hanover Street

Portsmouth, NH 03801–3912

www.heinemann.com

Offices and agents throughout the world

Library of Congress Cataloging-in-Publication Data
LeCount, David E.
    Dream writing assignments : 600+ prompts for creative writing / David E. LeCount.
        p. cm.
    ISBN 0-86709-557-1 (pbk.)
    1. English language—Composition and exercises—Study and teaching (Secondary)—United States. 2. Creative writing (Secondary education)—United States. 3. Haiku—Study and teaching (Secondary)—United States. I. Title.
    LB1631.L334 2004
    808'.042'0712—dc22   2003022504

Editor: *Lois Bridges*
Production service: *Colophon, Denise Botelho*
Production coordinator: *Lynne Reed*
Cover design: *Jenny Jensen Greenleaf*
Compositor: *Valerie Levy/Drawing Board Studios*
Manufacturing: *Steve Bernier*

Printed in the United States of America on acid-free paper
10 09 08 07 06 VP 2 3 4 5 6

This book is dedicated to our family, all of them—

my mother and father

My wife Arla, our sons: Jason, Joshua, and Daniel,

those I neglect as I write,

for no good reasons; and the ones who write,

or call to give me help and support:

Lois Bridges, Jim and Pat Hackett, Herb Kohl,

Mara Mills, Susan Ohanian,

and Denette Sauré, Lizelle Sauré,

Naomi Lee, Kristi and Lindsay James,

Amanda Craig, Rose Pendleton,

Brittany Philpart, Don and Betty Graves,

the Family of Lisa Ortiz, Bart, Anette,

Jeanette Bordy, Brian Fouts, Sophie Varga, Harvey,

Kuangkai, and our God-daughter, Estella Tai,

Christopher Tai, our youngest grandson;

To my brother Tom

Who lived too short a life

For no good reason

INTRODUCTORY NOTES

I

I am sitting on my deck with a former student who has brought her two young daughters for a summer visit away from the high-rise in which she lives in the winter with her husband. We have gathered blackberries enough for a tiny pie and a few plum cherries that largely were fed to our dog Harvey. The youngest will be six years old on September 11th of this year, and she is sitting on my lap as we write in languages other than English. I hold some lavender 3x5 cards out for her and she scribbles furiously with a calligraphy pen. When I ask what's she's writing, she responds, "It's my secret Eng-wish." Shortly afterwards, as I watch her drawing a globe and filling it in, I ask what she's drawing. She responds, "It's English as seen from a hot-air balloon."

One needn't go to another's children to find proof of their poetic imagination. When one of our sons was five and his foot fell asleep and woke up, he said, "Bubbles are going to come out of my foot." After returning home from school, another son said, "Sigh, my legs are boring." All parents who have been around young children know they are poetic and imaginative. I do not believe this faculty goes away; I believe it is taken away, and much to the detriment of our culture's time and place.

In the more than thirty years I have spent teaching high school English, I have seen creative writing classes offered and unoffered as often as music, art, and drama. Administrators were not quite sure what to do with such a class. Who would take it?

Who would teach it? What kind of credit would it be given? What would the grades mean? How would it fulfill state-mandated education standards? Would it help students with their SAT scores?

Many parents as well didn't want anything that might look like a "vague and easy class" on their child's transcript. Over the past twenty years, more or less, the competition for college slots has been desperate and fierce. Increasingly, it has been perceived as the only way to "make it" in tough economic times. *Rigor* (the sweating kind) was the word that had to be applied to classes for college-bound students. Anything that smacked of fun was viewed as a waste of time. The Puritan work ethic reared its ugly head and took over, and children lost their sense of innocent, imaginative play to become statistics of GPAs, SATs, and GREs. Students had to be doctors, lawyers, MBAs, things that were economically "realistic." And many of the college-bound students agreed with their parents. They were suspicious and downright wary of anything that wouldn't lead directly to an excellent career. And that career had only one route!

Meanwhile these same students responded to this ultimatum to become serious "things" by taking "drugs, sex, and rock 'n roll" to the nth degree. Later on, they rebelled with perversions of fun. Body piercing. Anorexia. Prozac. Gangs. Cheating on tests and homework. Plagiarism. Stress. Parents, politician role models, gave it to their kids, and their kids gave it back. Without outlets for fun and imagination, these perversions were perceived by children as fun, or, at least, unique identities. Play without consequences. And play with anger attached.

Einstein is often quoted as having said Imagination is more important than knowledge. Suspicious it is that the use of the imagination is fun and solves problems. *Creativity* increasingly became a dangerous Hippie word, not the defining characteristic of each new patent, each new Nobel Prize winner, each new spiritual insight, or each great work of art or music. Nonetheless, imagination was not seen as a great and humanizing problem solver. One of the arguments against it was that it was not practical in real life. Fun was not practical. It would not bring in a substantial income!

What might have happened if the FBI and CIA had been able to imagine themselves in guerrilla terrorists' shoes (call it *empathy*), and think what ordinary things in daily life could be put to use to cripple the United States. What if they had been able to think in metaphors and see a fully loaded airplane as a missile? To catch a terrorist you must think as one, but without imagination how can you have the empathy to be able to? To my mind, September 11 demonstrated beyond a doubt a failure of the imagination. As did the "tools" the Vietcong used against us. There is nothing frivolous about the imagination and the ability to think in metaphors. Nor is it practical only in war time. Surprisingly, it is the most practical skill of all.

Meanwhile, high school students spend most of their writing time with a five paragraph essay and formulaic writing from the outside in. At its worst, it can be writing with nothing to say. And it can invite students to hate writing. For the sake of argument, I would adopt the radical position that, to reword Einstein, imagination is more important than grammar. Students may have all the grammar lessons, five paragraph lessons a teacher can summon up, yet the magic of student writing remains in the discovery of a moment of wonder that takes the student away, and restores the play (fun) of childhood. Roughly paraphrased, Freud wrote that the goal of adult work was to recover the original joy discovered in childhood. (People who do not understand why *Don Quixote* is one of the world's greatest novels often miss this point.)

Many of the great writers have kept journals (not teenage "diaries") as a form of delight and discovery. But most of all as an exercise of the imagination to shape each day's meaning. And such journals can still be good therapy for children who are increasingly losing the innocence of childhood, the joy of play.

With good reason, many educators and writers argue that creative writing cannot be taught. And yet calculus is taught even though its immediate use is unclear. (It is difficult!)

Advanced Placement physics is taught and its immediate use is unclear. (But it is difficult!) Even if creative writing can't be taught, I don't doubt that under the right circumstances it can be encouraged, valued, resurrected, and, at the very least, not killed off. One might even argue that it is more immediately applicable and useful than physics or calculus. Yet how does it get a good student into Princeton or Yale?

The only alternative to a culture without imagination is a culture built on intelligence, practicality, materialism, class warfare, and corporate fraud. It is a culture drugged by television, diets, popular antidepressants, tabloids, disposable diapers, disposable people, and disposable marriages. (There is no better word to describe the twentieth century America than *disposable*. For people who are disposable are things, and things are simply tools, robots without empathy, who can neither love nor be loved, antidotes to meaningless pleasures, but nothing like simple fun. It is a culture without a soul, without a deep down spiritual meaning. It is a commercial for life. Not life itself.)

And it need not be that way. Though I do not believe these prompts can solve *all* of our culture's problems, I believe they suggest a place to start. Imagination can't be measured in time. A student may discover his own imagination in the blink of an eye. Suddenly one day the world is seen as round and not flat. Mold is seen as medicine. Life is seen as circular (reincarnation). Alas, students are seen as this year's "production models of 1400 SATs." The greatest wonder in the Universe is that there is wonder at all. That molecules could climb together, make us a brain to look back at the world with, imagining us as we imagine them.

Within each life (animal, vegetable, or mineral), imagination is embedded as surely as genes—or perhaps, as genes—to help each species change and grow and survive by use of the great *as if*. By its very usage, extinction by its very self can grow extinct. Students shove their way into my classes looking for meaning and afraid of finding none. What I believe they hunger for is ways that they can use their own memories coupled with imagination to make their own experience meaningful.

By reading and writing imaginatively, they can try on different sizes of self, different qualities of self until they either make one to suit them or discover one to suit them.

II

I did not begin teaching with these ideas about writing. Or if I did begin, I certainly didn't put them often into practice. Shortly after I got tenure I realized that I could use fun and enjoyable and silly writing assignments, and that what prevented me earlier was largely myself. As I gained confidence in my own imagination, my students also gained confidence in theirs. Furthermore, we began to share the stories of our lives, the meaningful events that made us who we were. We all had stories that were meaningful and when some were too private to be shared, I met with students at lunch not quite sure what to do but listen. Those who wanted more time, I invited over to our house for dinner and sometimes we talked into the late hours of the night. My wife and usually our oldest son floated in and out until bedtime.

In my education classes in college, I was admonished not to get too close to the kids because I could not grade them fairly. Or that I would not be able to discipline them if I did not keep my distance.

What if they called me by my first name? I was later told stories of students who got too close to their teachers and caused nightmares one way or the other. In fear, I asked my wife to stay close by when students visited me at our house. At school, I left the door open, and as often as possible had another student lurking about. I suspect now that most of this was based on my own inhibitions.

Over the years I learned I was modeling trust, and trust was probably more important between teacher and student than anything I could teach them verbally. I realized also that students wanted to learn from people they trusted, especially with regard to their personal writing. Good or bad, they didn't want to be graded by a computer, they didn't want to be known by their student number, they wanted to be taught by someone who was trustworthy and fallible. They wanted to be taught by someone who was a writer and reader himself, someone who had an identity and could discuss with them the qualities of their writing as one human to another. I found that by giving specific comments verbally was better than any grade I could have given them and was surely better than written criticisms in the margins of their papers.

III

In order to fight the battle against the imagination that I see pervading our society, I have offered within this book as many topics, ideas, tangents as I could to help a student play with words, possibilities, and discoveries. Many prompts are quirky; many require knowledge of other cultures or languages; all ask for curiosity. Perhaps they are scattered and disorderly. But ideas do not come to us as completed packages. Imagination is the force that drives each person's genius to create miracles. When imagination is not exercised enough, it withers as does the heart when it does not love enough, and miracles are not born. But it does not cease to exist. Its germ sits there, from childhood on, waiting to grow and be used again. It is the genie inside Alladin's lamp, hoping to be awakened. Waiting to perform wished-for miracles. Until we as a culture make explicit time for exercises in imagination, within schools and without, a part of our spiritual health, it will sit there like a vestigial organ, useless and withering. And so long as our culture values greed only, our children and students will learn nothing that is meaningful or useful in building a self.

IV

Note to Teachers: Usage

Many students across our country have been overfed on five paragraph essays, expository-this, expository-that, "what I did over summer vacation," What did Blake mean by line three?, sonnets, Shakespeare analysis, to the point they doubt their own imagination.

It is not, of course, that expository writing harms them. It's only when it's done to the exclusion of all other forms and optional shapes for thoughts. Only when the five paragraph essay excludes the possibilities for other forms. Or when the prompts themselves lack curiosity, spiritual and geographical dimension, practical use in the real life of teenage Americans, are the students harmed.

Advice to Teachers

1. Students should have freedom of choice regarding topics.
2. Many responses will require searches on the Internet.
3. Most prompts are designed for more advanced students in the eleventh and twelfth grades. Teacher's discretion is advised: TD-17 rating system.
4. Many Asian forms will seem strange to American students. Their art is less shaped by figurative language or strict forms, and is more about intuitive connections between nature and man.

Note to Readers

I have woven throughout this book examples of haiku, senryu, and tanka—all Japanese verse forms. In addition, I've included prompts that lead the reader to other masterpieces of Asian literature that I wish I had known about as an American student. I offer them for the curious as an introduction to alternative cultures.

Haiku seem to be favorites of American teachers. For this reason, I've included throughout some principles and examples that may help teachers approach this difficult form without resorting to the overly familiar 5-7-5 recipe. I am certain that students appreciate a short verse form that helps them heal and also express the meaning of each day's or moment's life.

In addition, they have helped me to practice living in the moment and discover sometimes hours, days, or years later what moments really mattered. They have given shape and form to moments of despair as well as moments of joy.

I have spread such forms throughout the book at intervals so the student writer is not overwhelmed by trying all bits of advice at once. For the bold and for those who do not wish to jump about in the book, I have made a brief list below of what is commonly the case in English language haiku.

Guidelines for Haiku

1. Haiku do not tell stories and are usually written in the present tense.
2. Haiku avoid figurative language like metaphors and similes.
3. Haiku rarely use abstractions, and avoid judgments.
4. Haiku rarely use personal pronouns like *I, we, you,* and so on.
5. Haiku are moments that take place in Nature, what is not man-made.
6. Topics and subjects need not express beauty.
7. Haiku have an implicit time and place, that is "summer forest."
8. Haiku rarely rhyme.
9. Haiku are often sentence fragments.
10. Haiku rarely ask questions.
11. Specificity is a must! (Daffodils not flowers, firs not trees, apples not fruit, etc.)
12. Haiku often unify implicit opposites.
13. Example:

> *summer shadow—*
> *Under the rose a toad*
> *Hides in its shape*

Guidelines for Senryu

1. Senryu are like haiku in that they are three lines, but unlike them in that their subject matter can be human-centered, implicit, social, or understated conflicts. (An old man at his wife's funeral notices a beautiful young woman.)

2. Senryu does not take place in Nature, but in human nature.
3. Suggestion: *Senryu* by R. H. Blyth is an invaluable book, but is out of print. Some used copies are still available.
4. Senryu treat human folly, offer an implicit criticism on a specific aspect of society, unlike haiku. (A woman is to go out on a date with a person she does not like, yet grooms for a long time anyway.)
5. Suggestion: www.haijinx.com/authors/e.stjacques.html
6. Senryu can involve humor, cosmic and comic.
7. Suggestion: www.reference.com/Dir/Arts/Literature/Poetry/ Forms_of_Poetry/Haiku_
8. Suggestion: www.nc-haiku.org/links.htm
9. There can be an element of irony, black humor. (An experienced race track driver crashes into a horse.)
10. Example:

Counting her change—
A penny is caught
In her palm wrinkle

Guidelines for Tanka

1. Tanka are apparently the ancestors of haiku in that they have the first 5-7-5 syllable pattern but with an additional 7-7 syllable pattern.
2. They are five lines long, and generally follow the line length pattern of short-long-short-long-long.
3. In content, they may be a cross between haiku and senryu.
4. Suggestion: www.worldhaikuclub.org/pages/resources_ websites-bio.html.
5. Suggestion: www.larrykimmel.tripod.com/links.htm.
6. Suggestion: *Japanese Linked Poetry* by Earl Miner.
7. Suggestion: Try a Web search for Chiyo-ni.
8. Example:

Two boys wade the tide
Till it chases them to shore,
And they chase it back—

Sleeping lovers in the sand
Wade deeper and deeper . . .

TO THE STUDENT AUTHORS

The questions in this small book are intended for the writer and the writer alone. There is no good reason or motive for forcing anyone into creativity or creative writing.

I say this for a very simple reason: It is very difficult to be stimulated or creative in an American classroom. Grades are involved and most of the beauties of nature that inspire people are not. Hard desks are not inspiring. Crowded classrooms are not inspiring.

I discovered that when I wrote at home, and let my imagination run wild, I was a much better writer. I doubt if many teachers understand how boring their classes are.

I found that only in privacy could I discover my own mysteries, and a voice that was distinctly my own. I hope that you may choose these questions as discoveries, as points of departure for finding your own voice. If you chose the right topic, you will write quickly and happily without criticizing yourself. Later on when you read aloud what you've written, you will hear the weak spots, and, as you change them, you will believe more and more in your own voice.

I do not know anything about you, but I do know you have a voice that will die if it doesn't get out. I do know that your Self and your story are as original as you make them. And I have always trusted my students to hold dear their own delight in writing.

Without that, what have you learned?

Discoveries

1. What kind of physical evidence would be necessary for you to believe in ghosts? What would your definition of *evidence* be?

2. How is the "top quark" like the "top dog"? How did the analogy come about? What kind of a metaphor is the *Big Bang?*

3. What is the personal value of being famous if it means most people care to watch you all the time and recognize you everywhere, but don't know you?

4. What is the Gospel according to St. Thomas? Why isn't it in the Bible?
See: *The Five Gospels* edited by Funk and the Jesus Seminar

5. Who is Kalidasa and why is he called the "Shakespeare of India"?
See: The Shakuntala of Kalidasa

6. Who invented down pillows and why? What were pillows made of originally?

7. What causes asthma? Why do doctors think it is dramatically on the rise? How is it different from emphysema? What is tuberculosis?

8. How was popcorn invented and why? Who invented it? Did he or she patent it?

9. At the first meeting of Bird Watchers Anonymous, what was done? How did the records that were kept read? What would their twelve step program consist of ?

10. How far back can the relatives of Confucius in China trace their ancestry? What would your family tree look like if you could trace your ancestry back that far?

11. What *ten* bumper stickers would you like to see and why?

What do you think a person's psychological profile would be who has the bumper sticker "Life is a bitch and then you die"?

12. What *five* classical composers of late nineteeth-century Russia turned away from western European influences? Why did they attempt to turn away?

13. Why do some doctors believe that warts can be controlled by the mind?

14. Why is it that cats need to be "put out" while dogs only need to be "let out"?

15. How did people preserve food before refrigerators?

16. Why is a *euphemism* for dying called "kicking the bucket"? It involves neither kicking nor buckets.

17. What is the male *synonym* for *wench*? What is the antonym for *wench*? What *connotations* make you think so?

18. Make a list and description of the *five* most humane zoos in the world and list what qualities you used to measure them.

19. Why were van Gogh's paintings relatively unvalued monetarily in his own time? What economic and aesthetic forces were at work when he lived?

20. Are there any "rebels" among your teachers? What are they rebelling against? How do you know?

21. What is the etymology of *oxymoron*? What value does it serve in modern English?

22. Which *colloquial* expressions have you heard recently:
   a. She has a bun in the oven.
   b. She was knocked up.
   c. He went off the deep end.
   d. He's one sandwich short of a picnic.
   e. He was chillin'.
   f. His company was downsized.
   g. He went to meet his Maker.
   h. She was as happy as a clam.
   i. She was in a family way.
   j. He looks like the missing link.
   k. He's as old as the hills.
   Which *ten* have you heard that are not on this list?

23. What are the *ten* most common movie clichés you remember?

   For example: A cliché can be a chase scene where the good guy's car never gets damaged or breaks down but the bad guy's car always crashes and burns.

Why do you think they have become clichés? What American cultural values do these clichés reflect?

24. Where do ethnic, racial, sexist, social prejudices, and slurs come from? Consider the following:

a. Asians are inscrutable and martial arts experts.
b. Jews are cheap and pushy/aggressive.
c. Blacks are lazy and violent.
d. Whites are dominating, rich, greedy, and snobbish.
e. Mexicans are hard workers good for stoop labor.
f. French are experts in love and romance and wine.
g. Germans are aggressive and warlike.
h. Intellectuals are useless in the practical world.
i. Women waste their time in college looking for a husband who will have money.
j. Boys in high school must be popular, athletes (muscular), or nerds.
k. Girls in high school must be Hollywood-sexy, popular, virgins but not *too* virginal.

25. Millions of people in the United States do not vote in Presidential elections. How does research explain that? In Australia, voting is mandatory. How would that be democratic or undemocratic in the United States?

26. Describe the different *connotations* for the following:

    a. tramps
    b. bums
    c. wayfarers
    d. homeless
    e. laid off
    f. disadvantaged

27. Who are the three leading profilers of serial killers? Briefly explain the theory of each one.

28. What conflicts do you imagine you would have if you had an identical twin? Are there support groups for twins? For triplets? Why would they need support?

29. What are the current methods of treatment for anorexics?

30. Interview a senior citizen for the purpose of determining his/her three favorite movies. Watch those movies and make a short list of notes on how they differ from your favorite movies.

31. The divorce rate in the United States is nearly 50 percent. If you had children and were considering a divorce, what would your top *three* reasons be to get divorced?

32. Are there too many lawyers in America? How many lawyers are there in France? In China?

33. Many people communicate their feelings as drivers by bumper stickers. What bumper stickers have you seen that communicate love? List five bumper stickers you have seen that express rage.

34. Consider the following argument: Women kill for men or men kill for women. Which argument makes more logical sense, and give *three* reasons why?

35. If you could control your baby's genes, which *three* genes would you wish your child to have? Why would you wish not to control his/her genes?

36. What is the etymology of the word *sex*?

37. Who are the ethnic minorities in your neighborhood? In what ways do they get along with each other?

38. Is the way that old people are treated in cold climates different from the way old people are treated in warm climates? How do you know?

39. What forces drive men to watch dogfights and bullfights in a controlled setting for money?

40. Why do women put on makeup that is known to be harmful to their health for the sake of looking "beautiful"? What *five* kinds of beauty can a woman have?

41. How are violence and intelligence related? What is the evidence?

42. Why are breasts so important in America that many women actually have silicone implanted in them to look great? What do "successful" implants mean?

43. What is your idea of the perfect experience of beauty or happiness?

44. Describe in *three* poetic lines what a turtle would look like without his shell.

45. If you were born as a cannibal on one of the outlying islands of New Guinea and grew up eating human flesh, what would be your favorite part and why?

46. Whose praise means the most to you? Why?

47. What religion has been involved in the most wars? How do you know?

48. If William Tell and Robin Hood had an arrow fight, who do you think would win? What motives would each have had, according to history?

49. How do pigs sweat? Be specific.

50. Who founded Sitka, Alaska? What was their purpose?

51. What is the meaning of the word *onomatopoeia*? What is the purpose of such a verbal ability?
a. What is the sound of a drunken eagle's wings flying?
b. What does the smell of a descented skunk sound like?
c. What is the sound of a frozen waterfall?
d. What is the sound of a yawning cat?
e. What is the sound of two mating salmon?
f. What is the sound of poppies closing up at sunset?
g. What is the sound of a hungry buzzard's stomach?

52. What is the *etymology* of the word *hate*?

53. Why do people recycle if recycle means to go around and around again?

54. What is a *euphemism* for:
   a. going to bed to escape without being tired
   b. buying something that you absolutely crave but absolutely do not need
   c. going on and off and on a diet again and again
   d. being in and out of therapy
   e. being politically incorrect
   f. "chick flick"
   g. the opposite of "senior citizen"

55. Are certain people more photogenic than others? If so, how can this be?

56. What does a new word have to do to be accepted for print in a major dictionary? What is your favorite word not yet in a dictionary, and what steps would you have to take to get it accepted?

57. Is the opposite of an antonym a synonym? Give *ten* examples.

58. What does the saying "You can't kill a disease by shooting its symptom" mean in the modern world?

59. Today people take pills for depression. Were people depressed in the past? If so, what did they take or do for it?

60. How do television and radio create the appearance of a whole separate community that is all-knowledgeable?

---

61. What is eating rice with one chopstick called? *Impossible? Chopsticks? Boredom?* Give *five* other possibilities.

62. What would you do if you were attacked in the morning by an alarm clock? Why is it necessary to be awakened each morning "alarmed"?

63. How many stomachs does a cow have? Why?

64. What actions might be involved in the "rite" to vote?

65. Why isn't *The Battle Hymn of the Republic* the national anthem? How did we get the national anthem?

66. When and why was the birth tax established?

67. What is taught in the School for Politicians? Not Answering the Question 101? What nine other classes?

68. Who invented the Hokey Pokey? Why?

LIKES: AN EXERCISE IN SPECIFIC DETAIL AND POSITIVE THINKING.

69. What are your favorite "likes"?
Examples:

* I like children who hold shells to their ears and listen to the tide.
* I like newborn kittens whose eyes are still glued shut.
* I like mushroom caps who survive after a hard rain.
* I like haloes around the moon.
* I like strangers who say hello happily with their eyes.
* I like the mystical feeling of early morning fog.
* I like the look of mussels on the wharf piling after the tide has cleaned them.

70. What caused the virtual disappearance of drive-in theatres?

71. Are snakes the only creatures with rattles? Why?

72. What do ghosts in ghost towns do for fun?

ADVICE COLUMN; "DEAR TABBY": WRITE A LETTER TO DEAR TABBY ASKING FOR:

73. The etiquette for declining invitations from cannibals.

74. Advice on how to deal with a grandfather who cheats at marbles when he is playing with his grandchildren.

75. Advice on how to gain sympathy for the five times in your life when you have had good advice and no one listened to you.

76. Instructions on how to gain respectability for the hobby of prune watching.

77. Advice on how not to go fishing in your neighbor's Koi pond.

78. Help on where to find side-saddle lessons for guys.

79. Advice on how to grow old disgracefully.

80. Advice on what to do if a stranger approaches you on a subway and offers to show you his pet frog in a greenhouse of your choice.

81. Advice on the prayer for a rich uncle who left you out of his will.

82. Advice to family whose son was suddenly shot to death on the streets who had no money to afford a funeral.

HEADLINES

83. Write the story for the following headlines:
* Local dog-knapper shot in his tail
* Fishing terrible this year in Death Valley
* Humming causes cancer, expert claims
* Two too or three times too many
* Ferret-keeper loses wife in mix-up
* Local sports teams insignificant, study shows
* Fleas can grow dogs to live on
* Local girl loses purse for 66th straight time
* Whorehouses closed this weekend for memorial
* Johnson's goat speaks aramaic
* Old man suddenly dies!
* Farmer hides his beehives from his wife
* Local beggar fined for begging again
* Local pastor calls wife "pagan with charge cards"

84. Why is America's national debt really never paid off? Who decides what the interest rate is?

85. If you found the Fountain of Youth and could live forever, would you? What *five* considerations would you use to help you decide?

86. What are your *three* favorite comedians and what sense of humor do you share with them?

87. Why do churches attract sinners? Do saints go to church? If so, why?

88. What items are contained within the Dead Sea Scrolls?

89. What are the *five* most important commands you can translate into "dog"?

90. What are the five passages from the Hummingbird's Bible that all young hummingbirds must memorize by heart?

91. What are the *Ten Commandments* for beautiful waterfalls?

92. Why do male emperor penguins raise their young?

93. Why do dogs chase their tails and cats do not?

94. What are the top five most beautiful birdsongs? Rank them in order of their beauty and explain your ranking in the language of a classical music review.

95. What is the American Civil Liberties Union? What three positions has it taken lately with which you disagree? Why?

96. To give permanence to their relationships, many couples exchange wedding rings, carve their initials into trees, get tattoos, or sign divorce decrees. What new ritual would you like to see that would signify permanence?

97. Irish Catholics have a wake as a funeral; Protestants have a funeral.

Describe the new ritual you would like to have for your funeral.

98. List *five* conditions under which someone might think taking drugs or committing suicide is a good option.

99. Briefly explain the evolution of the platypus.

100. What is the history of the Endangered Species Act? How did it get passed and by whom?

101. Who are five heroes to the people of modern day China? Modern day India? How can you find out?

102. Is anorexia contagious? What or who can people get it from and how?

103. Write the daily diary of a penguin at the South Pole who has no interest in weather reports.

104. Turtles move so slowly many people think they are stupid. What evidence is there that they are actually doing Tai Chi—moving meditation?

105. Some people are able to write one thing with their left hand and at the same time write another thing with their right hand. How do neurologists explain this ability?

106. What religions believe in nonviolence and actually practice it?

Are the Quakers a religion or a philosophical position?

107. Dogs have to have a license, in order to marry couples need a license—should candidates who run for public office be required to have a license? What should it measure?

108. What would a hippopotamus diet look like? What does one normally eat, and what would it look like afterwards?

---

109. Describe the childhood history of Sir Willful the Stupid.

110. Describe the ecstasy of a goose or duck in the rain. Use specific images and emotions.

111. What leaves "turn color" first in autumn? Why?

112. Who buried Grant in Grant's tomb?

113. What autumn leaves fall more slowly or more quickly than others?

114. Why do radical Right to Lifers try to kill doctors?

115. What *three* dreams are most popular for bears in hibernation?

116. How do the Chinese people avoid anorexia and heart attacks?

117. At what age do puppies learn best to obey? Why?

118. If there is a Society for the Prevention of Cruelty to Animals, why isn't there a Society for the Prevention of Cruelty to Humans to deal with the homeless, the impoverished, and the helpless?

119. Is there an absolutely perfect way to give directions to a stranger? Describe it in *five* easy steps.

120. On Valentine's Day, why is it that a heart symbolizes love?
Explain its history.

121. What therapy works best for a speedy slug? Give *three* reasons.

122. How can you put a fire out in a boat that you are in?

123. What is the explanation for spontaneous combustion? Can this happen to people too?

124. How can some people get hit by lightning and survive? What causes lightning to strike where it does?

125. In what *five* ways does racism hurt the person who has it? Is it contagious?

126. How can you tell the difference between Tongan and Samoan names by looking at them?

127. What is the Tasmanian devil's idea of Heaven?

128. If greed is an addiction, how can it be cured? What would a twelve step program meeting be like?

129. How does a funnel cloud form? What path would you like to take if you were one?

130. If there were a secret for every room of your house, for everyone who ever lived there, what would those secrets be? Describe each room and its secret.

131. What is the beauty of a housefly as described by another housefly?

132. Write a two hundred-word radio commercial meant to sell an imaginary product such as a Viaquack, and use *ten* of your own created words to extol its virtues.

133. Why does the English alphabet start with the letter A?

—◆—

134. The following words will only mean something after you give them definitions:

a. horsefilter

b. birdle

c. recackle

d. totaploat

e. plofludge

f. scanny

g. raisinserfle

h. mounge

i. protogrunt

j. defrocktile

k. noan

l. splission

m. goase

n. ombliminous

o. fundle

p. cowclapper

q. predung

r. Middlemummery

s. exghostify

t. splirred

u. roastate

v. swelch

w. triplegoating

x. beggicide

y. doozle

z. preobese

—◆—

135. Who invented the umbrella and list briefly his notes for the problem he was trying to solve.

136. Describe an animal you know personally that is the least lovable and explain why.

137. Describe an event in your life that was terrifying then, but that became merely "adventurous" later.

138. Describe a throat lozenge for a giraffe. What would its dimensions have to be in order to work for his sore throat?

139. Are pine needles leaves? Why or why not?

140. Some people say romance is dead in America. What is romance? Are women more romantic than men, or is that merely a stereotype? Why do you think so?

141. What made the Super Bowl so super? How does hype work and on whom does it work best? How do you know?

142. What is racial profiling? Is it new or is it only made to sound new? What is the difference between racial profiling and racism?

ASIAN LITERATURE

Japanese

143. Tanka #1

> *I open the window to let*
> *kitchen heat out into autumn*
> *moonlight and winds—*
> *perfume from your hair*
> *settles in my stillness . . .*

What is a tanka? Does this example follow the rules? Does that make it a good one or a bad one?

144. What kind of a thermostat do snakes have? How do they know where to get warm?

145. What *ten* ways can you use the expression "Don't that put a weasel in your bagpipe!"?

146. How do bald porcupines protect themselves when they grow old?

147. If snowflakes each have a different design, what are they designing?

148. What muscles, in particular, allow kangaroos to jump as well as they do and do humans have equivalent counterparts?

149. Do turtles ever have flatulence? How would scientists find out?

Tanka websites

1. Tanka

   Tanka. *History of Tanka*, Five Years of Tanka History in America, Jane Reichhold. Tanka for the Memory, Jane Reichhold. Tanka Article in Feelings, Jane Reichhold. *www.ahapoetry.com/tanka.htm*

2. **Gift of Tanka—Part One**

   A Gift of Tanka. Jane Reichhold. Copyright © 1990 Jane Reichhold. First printed in 1990. AHA Books, POB 767, Gualala, CA 95445, USA. – in *www.ahapoetry.com/giftank.htm*

3. **American Tanka**

   American Tanka News. September 27, 2002. Announcing Changes to American Tanka. It has been a joy to edit and publish American Tanka semiannually from Fall 1996.

   Category: Arts > Literature > Poetry > Forms > Haiku and Related Forms > Tanka. *www.americantanka.com/*

4. **What is Tanka? @ American Tanka**

   Home. What is Tanka? Tanka is the name of an ancient form of Japanese poetry. Tanka are 31-syllable poems. *www.americantanka.com/about.htm*
   www.asahi-net.or.jp/~mt1m-ootn

ASIAN LITERATURE

Japanese

150. Haiku(?) #1

Principle: Haiku photograph the moment's essentials with a lightning bolt, not a flash bulb.

> *Blowing sand—*
> *a poor dog sniffs it*
> *and sneezes*

Is this poem a *haiku?* Why or why not?

Resource:

Haiku Society of America

www.hsa-haiku.org/

151. Senryu(?) #1

Principle: A senryu displays the comic sadness and joy of all men.

> *homeless man—*
> *a newspaper both*
> *blanket and pillow . . .*

Is this poem a *senryu?* Why or why not?

References:

Haiku/Senryu

As I understand it, haiku are verses about nature and humanity written in a 5-7-5 Japanese syllable pattern, while senryu are haikulike verse, not necessarily 5-7-5.

www-personal.umich.edu/~troq/G

Senryus official website

1. *www.senryutheband.com/*
2. Haiku, Senryu, Tanka
   http://poetry.about.com/cs/haikusenry
3. *http://poetry.about.com/arts/books/poetry/msubhiku.htm*
   http://poetry.about.com/arts/books/po
4. Haiku and senryu harvest
   http://home.earthlink.net/~vgendrano/
5. Haiku or Senryu? How to Tell the Difference
   http://members.tripod.com/~Startag/Hk
6. Magazines publishing haiku, senryu, tanka, renga,
   haibun, *www.nhi.clara.net/hk004.htm*
7. Haiku versus Senryu
   At the simplest level, haiku are verse about nature and
   humanity, written in a 5-7-5 syllable pattern, while
   senryu are haikulike verse, not necessarily about . . .
   www.tnellen.com/cybereng/haiku
8. Senryu
   Ingrids Haiku-Welt. E-Mail: *ingrid@ingrids-haiku.de.*
   www.ingrids-haiku.de/senryu.htm

---

152. Haiku?

Principle: In a haiku all nature is beautiful; all nature is ugly.

> *starlight comes home*
> *on the back of a skunk—*
> *winter's stillness*

What kind of a poem is this? Why?

153. Make a list of as many kinds of love that you can think of. Then explain what, if anything, they have in common.

154. What three mushrooms are the most dangerous to eat? What exactly makes them poisonous to the human system? Do they have poison for the same reason snakes have venom?

155. Is the ability to concentrate an inherited trait or a learned skill? Do children in non-American cultures suffer from Attention Deficit Disorder? Do they have access to Ritalin? Adderall?

156. Haiku?
Principle: Haiku are like the spiritual split-second hand of an Eternal Clock but in words:
> *In what shallows*
> *Has the river flowed*
> *That it can be so clear?*

What is "wrong" with this haiku?

157. If you were a man forced to spend the night in a shelter for abused women, what would your night be like? What would your emotions be?

158. What is the psychological profile of women who dress in an overly revealing fashion and then complain of too much attention? How did they grow up? What were their families like?

159. What kind of power is fame? Does it involve comfort and security? If not, why do people want it?

160. Haiku?

Principle: Haiku has compassion and empathy for all nature, and loves them as fellow creatures who happen to share the earth.

> *Fallen leaves—*
> *a frog hides under*
> *and calls out . . .*

What is the implicit conflict in this haiku?

161. How do elk keep their antlers polished? Do they groom for the same reason cats groom?

162. What is the reason for road rage? Can rage be localized to one place and time? Journalists refer to airline rage, train rage, and so on. What does rage really mean?

163. Haiku?

Principle: Haiku often unite opposites and similarities.

snow—

moonlight

not the only show

What definition does this add to haiku?

164. Why are some old people kept in what are called nursing homes? Does the connotation imply that they are babies again?

165. List *five* reasons pigeons are attracted to statues for use as bathrooms.

166. Why do men who are out to kill wild animals refer to it as "going hunting"? Are the animals really wild? And are they really "hunting"?

167. Many drivers give their messages and personalities in America by way of bumper stickers. What message do you think is behind each of the following:

a. If you're rich, I'm single.

b. Life is a bitch and then you die.

c. He who dies with the most toys wins.

d. I'd rather be shopping at Nordstrom's.

e. My other car is a horse.

f. Proud parents of a _____ honor student.

g. Keep honking, I'm reloading.

  h. Better to be pissed off than pissed on.

  i. He who dies with the most toys still dies.

  j. Free Tibet.

  k. Anita Hill was right.

  l. You, out of the gene pool!

  m. Jesus was right.

  n. Trust the government? Ask any Indian.

  o. My honor student is dumber than yours.

168. Explain the origin of the expression, "To weird a whole line of sea cows."

169. Explain the origin of the expression, "Don't waste time beating your head over a nail with a screw loose."

170. What are *ten* practical uses for professional sunset painters?

171. Describe a piece of exercise equipment used in a weight-reducing salon for dinosaurs.

172. Write the lyrics for a hit CD that is a hate song rather than a love song.

173. Describe *ten* images that perfectly symbolize silence.

174. What famous lunatic proved the theory of gravity to be false by throwing an apple up at its tree until it stuck?

175. What ten trees are the most beautiful? Rank them in order, explaining your reasons.

176. How was the first electric sundial made? Who invented it and how was it patented?

177. Haiku?
Principle: A haiku does not narrate a story
> *an old stray—*
> *licks wounds*
> *all over*

Why is the word *stray* important to this haiku?

178. How would you tie your shoelaces in a way that would make them both more stylish and easier?

179. What *five* questions should not be answered?
What *five* questions have no answer? Why?
What is the opposite of a paradox?

180. Why are pigs the most intelligent barnyard animal? How can intelligence be measured? What is a pig's IQ?

181. Why is it that men in the world of fashion are stereotyped as being gay?

182. What *three* proverbs express the best summary of your life so far? What does each one say about your own experiences?

183. Have you ever felt that your life was "going too fast"? Describe the circumstances. How did it get back to a normal pace?

184. Write the lyrics to a country and western song as if it was written by a psychiatrist. What would the refrain line be?

185. If a caveman wrote a *sonnet* on his cave wall, what would the words be?

186. What personality type is needed to be a diamond cutter? How do you know? What training is required?

187. What are the *five* leading causes of insomnia as described by an owl?

188. Do ornithologists know if hummingbirds have favorite parts of flowers for eating? If so, what are they and why?

189. Do psychiatrists gossip with one another about their patients?

Write a short dialogue that depicts a brief gossiping session between doctors.

190. What group of people on earth lives the longest? What are thought to be the reasons?

191. What does a circus elephant think about while he is performing stunts required by his trainer?

192. Write down the Irish National limerick. Write a brief history of the limerick.

193. How do theoretical physicists understand the age of the Universe?

194. African Americans have joined together and broken free from the United States to form their own nation. Where would it be? What would its constitution sound like?

195. Many one-time role models for children have been discovered to have had checkered pasts. What brought them down if they were men? What brought them down if they were women? Do they have anything in common?

196. What do children of divorce most hate about the divorce? What kind of a survey could you make that would help you find out?

197. Are women as greedy in American culture as men? How could such a question be answered?

198. Is it within the powers of the Presidency to cancel national elections in the interest of national security? How do you know?

ADVERTISEMENTS

199. An advertisement: Primates in the zoos need to shave. Write an advertisement that sells an idea and a product to primates. Or a plan for dental care.

200. An advertisement to the homeless: The advantages of being in prison with three meals a day, heat, and a roof over their heads.

201. A biological advertisement for greed: Women store fat and husbands for lean times, and men store money to pay for lean times.

202. Write an advertisement for the spiritual beauty of the platypus.

203. Write an advertisement for a church that believes in corporal punishment.

204. Write an advertisement for frogs who have lost their voices and cannot find a mate.

---

205. Why do some people consider rape an act of violence and not sex? What is a profile of the typical rapist?

206. A clarinet is a reed instrument. What is the reason it uses a reed and what is a reed?

MYTHS

207. The Tower of Babel *myth* attempts to explain human differences especially with regard to why different people speak different languages. What would your myth be to explain the differences among human languages?

208. What *myth* explains the origin of human life?

209. What *myth* explains how human life existed on other planets before it came to earth?

210. What *myth* explains why some men are creators and others are destroyers?

211. What *myth* explains the sudden birth of Querkels on the fifteenth galaxy from our sun?

212. If van Gogh were born a composer and not an artist, whose music would his most sound like?

213. What are the *five* advantages of clay coffee mugs over plastic ones? Where does the best clay come from?

214. Some educators criticize schools because funding has cut out music and art programs. What music and what art would you like funded in your school and how much would it cost?

215. Why do few creative writers go into teaching in high schools?

———

THE NATIONAL DEFILER

216. What are the articles whose headlines are:
   a. Men from another universe located on Mars
   b. Cats experience post-partum depression after being spayed

c. Some lizards have five feet, expert says
d. Umbrellas not properly tested, consumer says, may sue
e. Slang helps the illiterate, expert says
f. Life after death may be the other way around
g. Superstar found not to be super

—•◦•—

217. What are the origins of "bride burning" in India? How did the custom come about and why is it continuing?

218. What is the Lunar Calendar that most Chinese use? Are there any calendars that begin "the new Year" in summer? What old man or woman began the first calendar?

219. What famous poet wrote "A Sonnet to Frogs"? How did it go?

220. Who invented American Sign Language? How does it differ from Indian sign language? Does anyone still speak Indian sign language?

221. Do languages other than English have as many homonyms? Where can you find out?

222. What is chivalry? Is chivalry dead? What is its history? Why would it be dead? What are its values?

223. Which is harder to train for riding purposes: a horse, a camel, or an elephant? Who would know?

224. Why do some people who smoke and drink live to be ninety years old and some people who smoke and drink die at forty? What factors determine lifespan?

225. How did used car salesmen get the image of "sleazy con-men"?

226. Why are blondes singled out in history for unusual qualities? What role does genetics play? What cultures value blondes to the extent of making them goddesses? How does Hollywood contribute to the image of blondes?

227. Is there such a thing as a gene for laziness? Who defines what is lazy?

228. Does your favorite teacher/professor challenge you most by what he expects, or by who he is?

229. Why do people have to sleep? Write a short history of the origins of sleep.

230. What language is the hardest to learn by a nonnative speaker? Why is it hard?

231. What daily activities are planned in the home for brain-different pollywogs?

232. Can a person with Attention Deficit Disorder ever become an explosives expert? A diamond cutter? What medications might make it possible?

233. Why did antidepressant prescriptions triple in the 1990s?

234. If a retriever goes skunk chasing, why is it a no-win scenario?

235. Are heroes born or are they made?

236. Describe the "shadowy cove of ignorance." What does the metaphor suggest?

237. What is the historical importance of soap?

238. Why do certain people always come late to parties and gatherings? What is their basic impulse?

239. "You cannot kill a disease by shooting the symptoms. You cannot kill terrorism with terrorism." What metaphor do these philosophical statements imply?

240. What are bio weapons? Are they legal or illegal? Who determines if they are legal or illegal?

241. In what part of the world is the venom of poisonous snakes outlawed? What kind of venom? Why is it outlawed?

242. In what states is capital punishment illegal, and corporal punishment by parents illegal?

243. What are three polite ways to correct a frog's croak accent that is not native to the creek?

244. Where is the orphanage for unwanted flamingoes located? What are the necessary conditions for diet and temperatures?

245. What famous spider was known as "the steel wool spider"? What did he/she add to the web to make it so strong? What constitutes an ordinary web?

246. Why do otherwise sane people love to eat eggplants?

247. What are *five* goals that a slug sets out for himself on a winter morning?

248. What *three* entries from Katherine the Great's diary do you find the most revealing? Write them.

249. We might all know who invented cell phones. Who invented *cell foams* and why?

250. How could anything truly go faster than the speed of light?

251. What exotic birds make the best talkers? Why? Can any of them be trained to be linguists?

252. What does *le crime fait la honte, et non pas l'échafaud* mean? Would its implicit morality be useful in the twenty-first century?

253. Aliens map the earth differently from earthlings. How do they draw their maps? By time/space coordinates? By colors? By size? How?

254. Twenty years from now will people bother getting married at all? What reasons will there be?

255. Haiku?

Principle: A haiku lives only in the moment when hummingbirds fly suddenly to a dead-stop in the air.

> *a robin trembles*
> *with the wire*
> *balancing his wings*

What unity is implicit with this haiku? What *ambiguity* does the second line create?

256. What *three* ways do your parents *embarrass* you the most? Do they know they're doing it?

257. What zoo animals are least comfortable with captivity? How is that measured?

258. How would tourism be affected in economic terms if the Eiffel Tower were leaning and not the Tower of Pisa?

259. What is the profile of a teenager who is most likely to commit suicide? Do you know anyone who matches your profile?

Is it always as unpredictable and unexpected as the media portrays it?

260. What war created the world economically and socially as the world you most know now?

261. If you needed a scholarship to go to college, would you lie in order to get it?

Would you lie in order to answer this question? How do lies function as a way of protecting ourselves, and therefore saving face?

262. Haiku?

Principle: Haiku need not have complete sentences.

morning fog
swells the backdoor slug—
the empty path

Explain what the reader learns from the last line.

263. Where does the phrase "I've got to get my beauty sleep" come from? What myth does it suggest?

264. What is the evolutionary purpose for the penis bone within walruses? What other mammals share this trait?

265. Someone once responded to the question, "Do you believe in ghosts?" with "What else is there?" Can a question truly be an answer to a question? What kind of values do you think that person had?

266. What do fawns do for fun? Write a short diary entry by a fawn that describes his/her day.

267. Why do people in the United States eat beef when bison is much more healthy?

268. If lobbyists in Washington were called "economic hit men," would their job be any different? How?

269. What is the evolutionary purpose of the skunk's form of self-defense by smell?

270. Can you recognize any constellations in the night sky? Which ones? How did you learn them?

271. Is beauty a part of the physical plant of your school? We have designer clothes; do we have designer schools? Why or why not?

272. What fish eat off the surface of the water and which feed off the bottom? How are they different?

273. If you were to write a love poem to your favorite pet, what would it sound like?

274. If the plural of *goose* is *geese*, why isn't the plural of *moose meese*? *Choose—cheese*?

275. Americans are universally agreed to be overweight. Why is this so? Describe your campaign to have

Americans fast two days a week to save food for the rest of the world and to become healthier.

276. Ask a fisherman to explain the difference between a bait fisherman and a fly fisherman. Describe his answer. Is there a class distinction?

277. Who invented the duck decoy? Or did he discover it accidentally?

278. What is the training of a truffle hound? A fishing cormorant?
Humans train other animals to work for them. What animals train other animals and what do they train them to do?

279. Describe the history of cosmetic surgery. How did it begin and why?

280. What does the proverb, "The man who chooses to read during the first day of spring can crush a robin's eggs" mean?

281. What are the four spices that you could not live without? How did you acquire a taste for them?

282. What does the word *seduce* mean? Is it an active or passive verb? What would be a verbal image of seduction?

283. What is an *epithet*? If you could give an epithet to *five* people you know well, what would they be?

284. Many dog owners groom their dogs carefully, daily. How do wolves survive in the wild without such attention?

285. What are the advantages of milking cows by hand? Interview a farmer or ex-farmer who knows.

286. Explain how a helicopter flies. Where does the air flow go?

287. What *five* words are most forbidden in your family? What words are the *least* heard?

288. Haiku?
Principle: Nothing needs to "happen" in haiku.
Fog lies
off the coast . . .
waiting for nothing

289. What makes people afraid to cross bridges? Can phobias be inherited? What new phobia can you think of that is not listed anywhere? (Do gophers fear earthquakes?)

290. What *five* ways can forks be improved?

291. Using the following pattern, make *five* animal nouns into verbs.
"He got *skunked*." Meaning: He was defeated horribly.
"Her laryngitis got *giraffed*." Meaning: She had a seriously bad sore throat.

292. Would Michael Jordan be a good basketball teacher? What skills does he have for teaching?

293. Why do most people remember Lincoln's Second Inaugural Address more than his First? What was different about his style?

294. Who invented the idea that frogs had warts? That cheetahs had spots? Using the same method, how would frogs describe humans?

295. In your opinion, what popular role model is least worthy of that designation? Why?

296. What water is the most pure? What does pure mean? Where can it be found?

297. What four nuns rebelled against "chastity, poverty, and obedience"? What imaginary revolution did they start?

298. Why are French people stereotyped as sexy and romantic lovers? When and how did this typecast begin?

299. If we were not here to observe them, would the stars still be light-years away? Away from what?

300. Of the *four* great haiku writers of Japan (Bashô, Issa, Buson, and Shiki), which is your favorite and why? Give an example of a haiku you think is especially meaningful to you.

301. What is amazing about the origins of the song *Amazing Grace*? How did its origin involve slavery?

302. Who invented the three-handled shovel for digging through especially tough terrain with the help of two others? Why didn't it sell?

303. Who was known as "The Human Skunk"? How did he or she earn the title? How did he or she prove worthy of a new and less ignominious title?

304. Briefly describe and explain the myth of the quick tortoise.

305. Do you have friends who are victims of divorce and friends who aren't? What would you say is the difference between the two?

306. Why are sunsets and waterfalls romantic? Why aren't lug-wrenches romantic?

307. What pain is the drug oxycontin trying to relieve?

308. Why or why not do you believe in angels?

309. What do you get when you cross the *National Enquirer* with the Congressional Record? Why?

310. What are the articles whose headlines are
   a. Man swallows own Adam's apple
   b. Zoo animals win class action suit
   c. Fern paranoia spreads in local village
   d. Steak with chocolate good for your diet
   e. Man with two arms finds another
   f. Wife shoots her hearing-aid off in argument
   g. Trojan horse look-alikes found on Mars
   h. Weasels don't suck eggs, farmer protests

    i. Women fear many things, study shows

    j. Skunks smell worse than first thought, boy says

    k. Old people tend to die, study reveals

    l. Some people don't like each other, Congress declares

311. Who lives the longest, bachelors or married men? Why?

312. Unscramble the following scrambled *proverbs* and explain what each one means.

    a. The early bird is worth two in the bush.

    b. Look before you leap changing horses in midstream.

    c. Hesitate and you are lost the straightest distance between two points.

    d. Beauty is in the eye of the it takes two to tango.

    e. Three's a crowd of the watched pot.

    f. Don't count your chickens before a stitch in time.

    g. One rotten apple ruins as the crow flies.

    h. A stitch in time saves a penny earned.

    i. To thine own self be true is not gold.

313. Name *three* prominent geographical features near your house and explain why you gave them the names you did.

314. Who do you least know and most fear? Are they the same thing?

315. There are debates about who wrote Shakespeare's works. Why are there no debates about who wrote da Vinci's notebooks?

316. In your family, who cares most about clothes and styles? How did it become that way?

317. What rocks are most fun to play with? Which rocks are best to throw? What physical properties allow you to skip rocks?

318. What does a tadpole feel like when he first realizes he is becoming a frog? What parts does he notice when his metamorphosis occurs?

319. Is it easier for you to understand a book or a movie about the book? Either way, why do you think it is so for you?

320. Explain the statement, "The great task of American culture is to reinvent the innocence of its children."

321. Have there been any Sasquatch sightings lately? Abominable Snowmen sightings? Have there been any sightings for the left-footed Giant Slug? Why do you think that the first two have something *elusive* about them?

322. What does the term "the village idiot" suggest? "The town drunk"? Why do these phrases sound dated?

323. What is the average cost for a psychiatrist in your town? A psychologist? A psychoanalyst? What is the difference in training? How can you pick a good one? Consumer reports? Has anyone you have known been through psychoanalysis? How did they "change"?

324. If you were in a disaster and unable to get to a store, what *five* plants in your yard would be safe to eat?

325. Haiku?
Principle: In nature, every thing living is equal in beauty, and its ability to be loved.

shallow spawning stream—
minnows too
must climb the stones

326. Is there a chemical in Redwood trees that keeps them from burning? If so, what is it?

327. How old is the oldest Bristlecone Pine? How do you count the ages of trees? How is history recorded in trees?

328. What is the *Tibetan Book of the Dead*? Is there an equivalent American Book of the Dead? Why or why not?

329. Did you ever read a review of a book or a film with which you completely disagreed? If so, pick one and explain using *three* examples why the review was wrong.

330. What do Daoist Chinese believe about the forces of yin and yang?

331. What *three* reasons might a ghost have to haunt your house?

332. It is the year 2155. Finally there is a pest control service for people. How do they operate?

333. What happens when skunks get together to party? Do they have a spraying contest? How do they socialize?

334. What vitamins or supplements do domesticated animals need?

Cats? Dogs? Horses? In terms of nourishment, what are the negatives for domesticated animals?

335. How are America's children spoiled with material possessions? How can children be spoiled with spiritual possessions?

336. Who is Cao Xue Qin? What great novel did he write? Explain briefly the plot of the novel.

337. What kind of a personality does the typical swan have?

338. Why did the Pony Express come to an end?

339. Many words in English are derived from Greek and Latin. Why do few students in the United States study Greek and Latin?

340. Write a sonnet that could have been written by a theoretical physicist that includes the words *quark*, *meson*, and *string theory*.

341. Explain the expression *El malo siempre piensa engaño*.

342. Explain the proverb, "The dirt does not understand the rain until it's mud."

343. Explain the superstition behind the expression, "Speak quietly of the weather, and it will not change."

344. *Elephantem ex musca facis* (L). How would this be translated into Spanish?

345. How do oysters breed? How are pearls made? If you were a pearl, who would your parents be?

346. What definitions can you think of for the following words:
- a. metaphor-proof
- b. stanzaless
- c. wirkfurmichfurfree
- d. wintles
- e. thirstthistle
- f. horricicanciones
- g. furmingler
- h. genocidiac
- i. indulgialantes
- j. swerzle
- k. anti-pearl

347. Tanka time

In her hair
a star braids its way
to the split ends—
the wind combs it
to her skull

What forces of nature act upon this woman's hair?

348. What makes darkness dark? Why does light travel?

349. What are three reasons that the Civil War should not have been fought? The Vietnam War?

350. Who first called the renaissance the "Renaissance"? What was the renaissance of your life so far?

351. You are to invent a new religion based on Wisdom. What *five* stages does the average human need to reach that final state of Wisdom?

352. Greed is a mental state of addiction. What would your twelve step program be for Greed Anonymous people?

353. Is pedophilia on the rise in America? Does anyone keep statistics on such things? What are the statistics?

354. What is the history of the word *merry* and why do we use it only at Christmas?

355. Which comes first, thunder or lightning? Why do people want to count seconds after lightning and find out the storm's distance?

356. What are the principles of feng shui? Why are they believable in this culture? Why are they not?

357. What are the top *three* reasons for divorce? Before you know the statistics, what have you imagined them to be? Can nations divorce other nations for irreconcilable differences? Why?

358. Respond to this quote: "When the Boeing jets hit the Twin Towers, Americans felt their own grief had been trivialized by comparison. What grief did the air traffic controllers express?!"

359. Suddenly Similes (What qualities are being compared?):
   a. smirk *like* a weasel
   b. reach out *like* a four-armed beggar
   c. pray *like* a fiend
   d. hop *like* a one-legged frog
   e. creepy *as* a no-legged snake

    f. spending *like* a bankrupt wannabe

    g. dream *as* the glorious dream

    h. sleep *as* a wino sleeps

    i. He was like the animal left out of the Ark

360. Momentarily Metaphors (What qualities are being compared?):

    a. She bankrupted her own children

    b. He chased the tail of his own thought

    c. More wind in his voice than words

    d. Homelessness is a symptom, not a disease

    e. He got hosed

361. What do turtles do for fun? How does an objective observer know when they are having fun?

362. Why does skinny-dipping sound like an old-time activity?
How would you feel at a nudist colony and why?

363. What qualifies a person for the Nobel Prize for Peace? What do you have to do?

364. If you were born into a race and could stay only in one race throughout the history of civilization, what race would you choose? Why?

365. If you could be born and live in a century other than the twenty-first, which would it be and why? What habits of life would be more appealing?

366. Why are there fewer Emperors, Kings, Queens, Counts, and members of royalty in the current century than in the past?

367. What logical system of thinking is the Braille alphabet based on? How did Braille come into being?

368. Are worms blind? How do they know how to get home?

369. Who invented wind tunnels and why?

370. Who were the original "Architects of Snowflakes" and how did they come up with so many wondrous patterns?

371. Haiku?
Principle: Haiku do not make judgments or criticisms.
> *a late dawn—*
> *the winter rooster*
> *is my friend*

What connection with nature and its habits does this suggest?

372. Why are groups of cattle called "herds"? What are groups of hummingbirds called? Herds of elephants?

373. What are the personality differences between dinosaurs and dragons?

374. If two gangs are competing to steal a gem, what are the ethics and protocol of behavior when they meet?

375. What makes whales mammals? Why does it seem strange that they are mammals?

376. Who licensed his pet turkey when Thanksgiving was coming around? What do you have to fill in for a pet turkey license?

377. If men were more womenlike, what emotions would be different? If women were more menlike, what emotions would be different?

378. If "home is where the heart is," where is your home?

379. Why are television commercials more effective when they're annoying than when they are funny and creative? How can you find out?

380. If bullfrogs were domesticated and housebroken, what *five* tricks could they be taught to do?

381. What was it about Bach that was unappreciated in his own time? Is it possible that he will be unappreciated again in the future?

382. Who wrote *Daesop's Fables*? Write an example of one that illustrates why they were inferior to *Aesop's Fables*.

383. When criticizing American literacy, many social critics suggest that "print is dead" and that Americans are a postliterate generation. If this is so, how can it be resuscitated? Why should it?

384. What *five* sporting events are most watched in the turtle Olympic games?

385. What is the *one* eternal proverb that will always be true in the past, present, and future? Why do you think so?

386. What is the English proverb equivalent to the Spanish proverb *el río pasado, el santo olvidado*? What truth do they have in common? Does it also rhyme in English?

387. If you were to live within Dickens' *A Christmas Story*, who would be your ghosts of Christmas past, present, and future?

388. English requires a word that means a group of, such as "a school of fish," "a herd of cattle," and even "an exaltation of larks." What would the following grouped animals be called and why?

  a. vultures
  b. stingrays
  c. kangaroos
  d. hippopotamuses
  e. mosquitoes
  f. horned toads
  g. tarantulas
  h. lice
  i. pimples (as in, She had a herd of pimples on her face.)
  j. cacti or cactuses
  k. cockroaches

389. What do songbirds do when their young are song-illiterate? What teaching methods work best for birds?

390. Why do fish swim upstream to spawn and not downstream? Downstream would be easier.

———◆———

391. Write the text for one of the following headlines:
  a. Man discovers own toes at end of feet
  b. Life on Mars found to be stupid, IQ tests show

c. Kissing warts can cause frogs, research shows

d. Snakes shorter when they curl up, vet says

e. People laugh at comedy, research reveals

f. Why kangaroos cannot dance, the inside story

g. Even kings get jock itch

h. Happy people on the decline in america

i. Sometimes people remember dreams after sleeping

392. Where do cannibals live? Why are there fewer cannibals in New York City?

393. What is the prayer devised by the Homeless People of America?

394. Write the notes of the inventor of toilet paper. What spurred his act of creation?

395. Who was the Fourth Musketeer who was left out of the story? Why was he left out?

396. "Men drink so as to forget the criticisms of women: women eat chocolates so as to forget the criticisms of men." Agree or disagree with this statement and explain why.

397. Who won the Cat Tree Climbing Championships in northern Alberta? What special skills did the cat exhibit?

398. What would men be like if they actually experienced Men-o-pause?

399. Suddenly Similes (What qualities are being compared?):

    a. She ate *like* a house full of beggars.

    b. He was as hyperbolic *as* an oyster full of pearls.

    c. His muscles were *like* limp noodles.

    d. He was as quick *as* an otter on ice.

    e. Her sadness filled the room *like* an ancient smell.

    f. She was as slippery *as* footsteps on moss.

400. What holds glue together?

401. What is more intoxicating: love, fear, or power? How would you know? Is it linked to one sex or the other?

402. What chemical element is so powerful in a skunk's scent that it radiates everywhere and makes other animals fear it?

403. Why do people need sleeping pills to sleep, and coffee and alarm clocks to wake themselves up? Can't people learn to trust their senses?

404. Who were "The Hollywood Ten"? What did they do, or not do? What happened to them?

405. Who invented the sin dial? All you need to do is type in your suspected infraction on the Internet, your age, sex, and religion—and it tells you on a scale of 1 to 10 how bad you've been and how to remedy it. What intricate problems did he/she have to deal with? (Completely confidential)

406. Why do elephants have such long tusks and yet such relatively small mouths?

407. What do you imagine the conversation is like between two highway patrol officers just getting off duty after an uneventful shift?

408. Is *Evil* in *Axis of Evil* an Old Testament word or a New Testament word? How can you find out? Why do Christian fundamentalists believe in the Old Testament God, and not the New Testament God?

409. How do cattle know—if you were one of them—where human border crossings are?

410. Make a short list of slang words (six) used for the opposite sex in your neighborhood. *Hunks, chicks,* *dudes, rogues, babe,* and *fox* could be some. Explain the connotation of each and the origin. Are there more slang words for males in your community?

411. How did Lawyerphobia become a massive problem in the year 2250? What *three* historical events led up to it?

412. Some words die. Can the word *discreet* be used any more? If so, give *three* ways it could be used accurately.

413. Playing bugles seems to be on the decline. Where do you need to go to learn to play the bugle?

414. What is the *Horn of Plenty?* Where did the Horn of not-Plenty come from? Why did it come into use?

415. What is the history of wearing white at funerals in China? What color do people in Tahiti wear?

416. Why do English teachers teach vocabulary words that are no longer in use? Does it have to do with doing well on the SAT?

417. Where do dogs go for the purpose of having their masters better trained? What dog support groups exist in their neighborhood?

418. The month of January 2002 was the hottest on record. Why?

419. Where can you find the largest frogs in the world? What conditions are needed to allow them to grow so large?

420. What fashion models show serious signs of physical self-neglect? Who are they and what are the signs you first notice?

421. Why are robots important? For cheap labor? For prestige? Due to human laziness?

422. What is the English equivalent of the Spanish proverb *fuése por lana, y volvió trasquilada?*

423. Which presidents have used speech writers and which have not? When you use someone else's words on a term paper without giving proper credit, it's considered plagiarism. How is this principle different for presidents?

424. Haiku?
Principle: Haiku rarely use metaphors or similes, but this one does. Why?

> *doe laundry—*
> *she licks her fawn's spots*
> *whiter and whiter*

425. In America, what is equivalent to knighthood? A politician? A rock star? What would any noteworthy American have in common?

426. Respond to this statement: "In times of insecurity people avoid taking risks when it should be just the opposite—risky times require actions that don't guarantee security."

427. Should *The Gulistan of Sa'di* be permitted in your high school library? Why or why not? What about *The Perfumed Garden*?

Are there any equivalents to these titles in American literature?

428. Why is it that Mt. Kingwashiguchi has never been climbed?

429. What do practitioners do for fun at the annual convention of Accupunctureneers?

430. In the great but unknown myth "The Stealing of Truth," who stole it? What plans did they make? Why?

431. How many concentric universes are there? Why do particles move circularly rather than linearly? Are explosions eventually circular?

432. In the opera *The Marriage of Figaro* by Mozart, who was the author of the libretto? What else did he do? Why is he less famous?

433. What *three* things does the unknown legend of the *Unremembered Turtle* predict for the future?

434. What causes elephants to go to a great graveyard? Do they sense death coming?

435. Why was Tchaikovsky's first ballet *Swan Lake* such a failure that it took him nearly ten years to write another?

436. What is the sport curling? How is it played? Who invented it?

437. For what did Rabindranath Tagore win the Nobel Prize? What is his book *Gitanjali* a collection of? Why was W. B. Yeats interested in him?

438. What causes human hair and nails to grow even after death?
    What biochemistry is involved?

439. How many saints in America have been canonized by the church?

440. What do *delusions* and *illusions* have in common?

441. In what cultures do women and men wear hats? In what cultures do men only wear hats, or women only? What is the history of the hat?

442. What do transvestites and politicians have in common?

443. Tabloid Tales. Write a story to accompany these headlines:
   a. Lost man finds grave his own!
   b. Court rules Venusians have rights to Saudi oil fields
   c. Old people often misplace things, survey shows
   d. Angry husband sees mother-in-law on wife's behind
   e. Bees do poorly in spelling bees?
   f. Expert decrees most women look better in clothes at office
   g. Man with two heads donates one to charity!
   h. Hangman in Montana caught in dying business

444. What film is the greatest Western ever made? What values does it teach? What considerations make it the best?

445. What do most famous people do after they've been famous? Are there any studies on the effects of fame?

446. In what ways was Gandhi influenced by Henry David Thoreau?

447. Describe your reactions poetically to a rejection by a boyfriend on a dream date.

448. Proverbs:
   a. Loneliness starves more than hunger.
   b. In pages are words; in life are endless seconds.
   c. Only owls know who.
   d. Man kills his own kind without starvation.

Based on these four models, write *four* of your own.

449. Tanka Time

> *she combs her hair*
> *from one side to the other*
> *and back again . . .*
> *In the moonlight I know*
> *beauty she never will*

Who is the speaker in this tanka? What is the implicit conflict?

450. If you had to lose a finger in an accident, which finger would it be. On which hand? Why?

451. Who wrote Aesop's Foibles? What *three* stories did they tell and what were their morals? What animals were used as characters?

452. Why was the pillow designed with four corners and not three like a triangle?

453. Where is the largest modern library in the world? Where were famous libraries of the past and what was their fate?

454. How do cacti reproduce? What enables them to live in the relative absence of water? As the world dries out due to global warming, will people live like cacti?

455. What substance makes frogs' eggs cling together? Where does it come from?

456. What does the French proverb, *Il faut souffrir pour être belle* mean in English? What idea of beauty in America is not in this proverb?

457. What Shakespearean play gives the best dramatization of the notion that revenge is self-destructive? In what ways? Why?

458. What modern musical is the most descriptively accurate in its depiction of the values of American culture? Consider: *West Side Story*, *Oklahoma*, *Cats*, *Porgy and Bess*, *Evita*, and so on. Are Broadway musicals dying?

459. Write *five* country and western song titles based on the following:

    a. Lonely in the wind says my tractor.
    b. Roundups make me tired of tired.
    c. I drank all cowboys under the table.
    d. What's my saddle doing in another man's barn?
    e. Wind is the name of my face.
    f. She drank the train dry, why?
    g. My bridle's on you but my saddle ain't.
    h. I got cactus in my chaps.
    i. Outta jail and happy as a quail.

460. What are the plans for the faith-based missile defense system modeled after?

461. Before Lincoln gave his *Gettysburg Address*, who spoke and what did he say? What was his response after Lincoln spoke?

462. How can rifles be ordered by mail? Can the ingredients for fertilizer bombs be ordered by mail? Do you need to know the answer to these questions?

463. Will there be a need for shoelaces fifty years from now? If not, what will replace them?

464. What *three* issues, comments, or actions make your parents most angry? Why?

465. People fear the world is becoming impersonal and depersonalized. When someone says, "It's none of your business" or "Mind your own business" how does the connotation of the word *business* reflect economic relationships rather than personal relationships?

466. Why did many great writers/thinkers become expatriates? Consider Hemingway, Ezra Pound, Einstein, and so on.

467. Who invented the system of noncounting? It involved the theory that nothing that could be counted mattered. How did it change the qualifications for the Nobel Prize in Economics?

468. What *three* paintings by van Gogh would you want to remember forever? Why?

469. What nation's women have the most beautiful hair? Why?

470. What words would you like to have said at your funeral?

471. How do bears sleep and hibernate without waking up? How does their body chemistry change?

472. Why do cowboys wear chaps?

473. Who was referred to as the "lost ballerina?" What did she do?

474. How do blind people count change?

475. What *three* tricks do turtles do at a magic show?

476. What stomach aid do termites take after a bad meal? How does it work?

477. How would slugs have to be redesigned in order to be able to jump?

478. Tanka Time

> *He sweeps the steps*
> *out of loneliness,*
> *not cleanliness—*
> *her voices flees*
> *and flees with each stroke*

Why is the word *flees* repeated?

479. Write the text for the following headlines:

    a. After years of searching, professor finds slippers on own feet

    b. Blonde wins spelling bee with word "kat"

    c. Mother of serial killer doesn't like serials either

    d. Family horse puts saddle on man

    e. Email from space warns of great distances

    f. Ghost dies and leaves body to science

    g. Coloring books easier to read for most kids, expert says

480. Can blind musicians learn new music by Braille? How do they read it?

481. What is the average weight of a female elephant? How does it compare with a male elephant? Do female mammals generally have a greater degree of fat than males? Why?

482. What is the history of the word *mill*? *Steel mills*? Why is the word no longer in use?

483. What snake sheds the longest skin? How did you find out?

484. Why are the following headlines significant? (Answer *five*)

a. Mozart's grave found
b. Beethoven's Tenth Symphony astounding!
c. Amelia Earhart's daughter doing well
d. Will Rogers in nursing home
e. van Gogh's ear found
f. DNA from frozen caveman successfully extracted
g. Einstein's sperm donation found
h. Hitler DNA can be cloned
i. Jimmy Hoffa doing well
j. Arranged marriages more successful

485. What *ten* messages can you leave on your answering machine that will express the imagination you possess?

a. The occupants of this house have been abducted by three Martian masseuses, we'll return your message when we feel better!
b. No one in this house has died today. But leave your message as if someone has, in a soft and grief-stricken voice.
c. Leave a message if I left my shoe at your house last night. Leave another message if I didn't.

486. In very poor countries, what do thieves steal? In very rich countries, what do thieves steal? What is the difference?

487. What is the worst recipe for a meal you can imagine? Include *four* ingredients. Give it a name.

   a. Glazed chocolate maggots in a cream sauce

   b. Oyster flavored ice cream followed by mints

   c. Pâté de foie gras á la mode

488. What is the difference between fast food and slow food? Why did fast food originate?

489. What does the Latin *ex nihilo nihil* mean? What kind of metaphysics does it express? What theory of creation does it comply with?

490. What is the difference in price between a first edition, autographed copy of a book and a later edition, unautographed. Give *five* examples. See *www.bookfinder.com*.

491. How is it that anger allows someone else to control you?

492. Who were the authors of the book of *Genesis* in the *Bible*? Why do Biblical scholars think so?

493. Haiku?
Principle: Haiku almost always use the present tense.

Spring cleaning—
new grass
washes with dew

What is being personified in this haiku? What are the haiku rules about personification?

494. Some people who procrastinate are great achievers. Who are some of history's great procrastinators? Why do people procrastinate?

495. Haiku?

Principle: There can be an intuitive connection between lines.

still moonlight—
she fans her face
with one hand

What does the verb *fans* in the second line add to this haiku?

496. In India, which dialect is most prevalent? What authors have spoken it?

497. Is it possible to know what languages died out because no one spoke them any longer? What language did Ishi speak? What ten Native American languages have died out?

498. Why don't women worry about going bald as much as men seem to?

499. What is the history of gum chewing in the United States?

500. Who invented pockets in pants? Who invented knitting? Is it possible to know?

501. Is helplessness an addiction as much as power is? What kind of support group would be needed for each?

502. What is your typical profile of a stamp collector? What are people like in general who collect things? How do antique collectors and human head collectors differ?

503. Some people argue that the printing press made pornography available to the masses. How did video change that? How did video alter the images of women? And of men?

504. Who won the first (and last) Bowling-with-Skunks championships? What were the rules of the game?

505. What would you want as your last supper if you were a prisoner on death row? Why?

506. Do upper-class people or lower-class people go to the zoo? How can you know?

507. Why do some older men prey on younger women? Is it fear of growing old, death, powerlessness, or something else? Is it common only in the human species? In what other species does it happen?

508. Do lower-class people go to libraries? Operas? Symphonies? Movies? What other opportunities does expense separate the classes in the United States?

509. Why do thoughtful and intelligent women date married men? How can they hope to benefit? Or succeed?

510. People say "Beauty is only skin deep." In our culture, what other kind of beauty is there? Where can one find beauty that is not "skin deep"?

511. How do you play the game Chase the Weasel in the Catacombs? Where is it popular?

512. Can people actually die of loneliness? If so, what happens within their biochemistry?

513. Making Lists

    a. How to enjoy telemarketers:
       In your best foreign accent repeat again and again the phrase, "My shoe makes my toes feel like sandals."

    b. How to reply to beggars:
       Repeat loudly and firmly, "My voices keep telling me no."

    c. How to respond to an officer who pulls you over and asks for your driver's license:
       "My co-pilot thinks you're a whistle."

    d. How to respond to someone who wishes you to have a good day:
       Pantomime the throwing of your imaginary hat in the air.

    e. How to respond at a concert or gathering where clapping is expected:
       Repeat the Sanskrit and sacred Tibetan OM five times in a row gradually raising your voice.
       Make a list of your own *five* imaginary solutions to difficult situations.

514. Who built the Great Wall of China? Who built the Tiny Wall of China? How did it get forgotten? Historically, what has been the fate of walls as dividing lines? (Compare: the Berlin Wall, Frost's "Mending Walls")

515. Make a list of *five* things the average citizen could do to make a change in prisons and the humane treatment of inmates.

516. In the Civil War both sides had to eat.
What was the favorite food of the North?
What was the favorite food of the South?
What would each have preferred to eat?

517. In Operation Desert Storm, what did American soldiers do for love? In the war in Iraq, what did soldiers do for love? In what ways do war and love go together? Do soldiers often marry women they love in foreign countries?

518. If you worked for Suicide Prevention, what *ten* phases do you wish you could say most soothingly?

519. Proverbs. How would you translate these proverbs into an English proverb of the same meaning? What dictionaries would you need? Which one is the phony proverb?
a. *el hijo del tigre nace rayado*
b. *el tiempo es oro*
c. *durch Schaden wird man klug*

    d. *gato escaldado d'agua fria tem medo*

    e. *insanus omnis furere credit ceteros*

    f. *I no uchi no kawazu*

    g. *ni firmes carta que no leas, ni bebas agua que no veas*

    h. *Las Frogas no hablan conmigo ahorita*

    i. *nimum ne crede colori*

    j. *è cattivo vento che non è buono per qualcheduno*

    k. *zhi qi ran bu zhi qi suoyi ran*

520. How can you know which wild mushrooms are safe for eating? Would you trust a friend to tell you?

521. Did you ever have an idea or poem that sounded great as you wrote it down at bedtime only to discover that when you woke up it sounded terrible? What accounts for the difference in perception?

522. Suddenly Similes! Which is the most vivid for you and why?

as cozy *as* a snail in shell

fat *as* a cake store lady

she looks *like* the end of the rainbow

he looks *like* he fell off of a truck

daffodils *as* yellow as a finch

as fired up *as* a snortin' bull

concrete that grows *like* a weed

she loved *like* a firefly, not a steel girder

523. Haiku Interruptions

Principle: Haiku don't usually have an "I" speaker in the lines.

> *fade gently into the silence*
> *O pine-blown moon—*
> *I am only me*

What does the second line suggest about the moon?

524. Haiku?

Principle: Haiku connect man with nature when they seem separate.

> *The monk's prayer*
> *on a chilly morning:*
> *a breath's cloud*

What unity within nature is suggested in this haiku?

525. How is it possible to count frogs' eggs?

526. What would a haiku sound like if written by a lawyer or tax accountant?

527. What *five* qualities are essential for a great teacher?

528. What *five* fears create insomniacs of turtles?

529. Why do men wear socks and ladies wear nylons?

530. How do the lenses in telescopes work?

531. If named only after constellations, what would the seven days of the week be?

532. How many seasons are there on Mars? Why?

533. Do ghosts believe in ghosts? How can we know?

534. Who created unicorns? Why weren't they "dualicorns"?

535. What is more likely to be in a Chinese diet: fish, beef, or chicken? Why?

536. Why were the following dinosaurs left out of the books on earth history?
   a. whineosaurus
   b. blindfootopolis
   c. sneakosaurus
   d. sloppyosaurus
   e. floatoplatypus
   f. oysterosaurus
   What *five* could be added to this list and why?

537. What film (movie) presents the proper or best relationship of love between the sexes? Why?

538. What film depicts the ideal man to you? Is he also the ideal husband? What film depicts the ideal woman to you? Is she also the ideal wife?

539. Why was Naguib Mahfouz blind? Who was he and what did he do?

540. How would you describe your earliest memory of reading? Of writing for fun?

541. Tanka Time

In silence she waits
at the window sill
for sun to set—
Her aging hands warm
in dirty dishwater

What implicit connection is made between the woman and the sunset and the waiting in this tanka?

542. What features did the proto-Yoyo lose when the real yoyo came out?

543. Why is it that girls played Jacks but guys didn't? What skills were involved? What games helped you understand and define what you were good at?

544. What *five* ways do you imagine you could express more kindness in your own life? And to others?

545. When did you first become aware of the length or shortness of time? Not time on the clock necessarily, but the loss of a friend or a parent or a pet or an absence from home?

546. Who wrote the *Songs of Kabir*? What do they try to express?

547. Who was the creator of the Motown sound? In what way does it reveal the history of music in America?

548. How did Tina Turner become a pop star and for what is she famous?

549. What song or piece of music do you think you will still remember when you are fifty years old? Why? What do you associate with it?

550. What *three* things prevent snakes from being able to whisper?

551. What is a turtle's idea of Heaven?

552. What *five* aerobic exercises do turtles do?

553. What is the correct method for lifting a deadly poisonous snake?

554. What kind of a person invented the Glockenspiel?

555. What *five* events are most competitive in the sloth Olympics? Add *five* of your own to the following list.
    a. Zen meditation and tree climbing
    b. slow dancing
    c. lazy mating
    d. sleeping to death

556. How would you improve on modern competitive sports to make them more personal?

557. When scientists say a whale weighs such and such pounds, how do they know? How do you weigh a whale?

558. What changes would you make in your lifestyle if you knew you were immortal?

559. Did Americans invent blues, rock 'n roll, and jazz? What radio stations where you live play classical music?

560. What does the Constitution say about the difference between a *conflict* and a *war*?

561. What country's population suffers the most from insomnia? What organization would keep such statistics?

562. Why can't people as loving friends be pain-killers rather than drugs?

563. What would be the mottoes for the fifty states if you could make them up?

564. What does the Islamic world think of Rumi? Who is Rumi? What language did he write in?

565. If you read Sanskrit, what *three* works would be essential to you in order to understand Indian culture?

566. Some people believe lawyers are taking advantage of the chances for frivolous lawsuits. Using the following signs as examples, what other *five* warnings might you see for such a practice?
  a. Don't put lips in elevator doors!
  b. Don't slip stealing coins from the fountain!
  c. Warning: Slow waitresses!
  d. Gorillas can be unfriendly.
  e. Motel sign: Soap may be too slippery for old people.
  f. Do not use hairdryer in bathtub.
  g. Warning: Do not sharpen this chainsaw when it's running!

   h. This tollbooth keeps no cash!

   i. The batter is not responsible for foul tips.

   j. This car may not drive safely after the first rain.

   k. To tourists: This waterfall may not be at its best when viewed during an earthquake.

   l. Warning: This rocking chair moves back and forth.

567. It has been discovered that 20 percent of California's children live in poverty. Describe a day in the life of one of these children.

568. Is the following a tanka? Why or why not?

After the storm
the pine needles
paint with wiper blades
Here and there
the wind and fury left behind

569. The Supreme Court has been trying for years to determine a working definition for pornography. What would your definition be and what arguments would it be based on?

570. If a movie were to be made of your life thus far, who would play the starring role? Why? Would it be a tragedy or a comedy and what would its rating be?

571. Many people believe in and stories depict the magical properties (and power) of hair. Samson and Delilah. Rapunzel. Men and women spend millions of dollars at the barber or hairdresser. Many men shave off their natural face hair; most women shave off their leg hair and underarm hair. Women pluck their eyebrows; old men trim their ear hair or nostril hair. Is this a stage in evolution or a modern fad that will change with time? Why do you think so?

572. Why is it that old clothes feel more comfortable? Who helps you decide what clothes you wear, and, if no one helps you, how do you decide? What goes through your mind when purchasing a new item?

573. Very few people in the United States are harmed by spiders. In fact, relatively few people worldwide are harmed. Why does it seem so many people suffer from arachnophobia? How do phobias develop?

574. Tabloid Telling

Write the stories that would explain the following tabloid headlines:

a. Student commits suicide after getting all As
b. Homosexual suburban rats on the rise
c. Weasels cannot afford orthodontists

    d. Ugly people can't afford cosmetic surgery. How about you?

    e. Last Civil War veteran reincarnated, guru says

    f. Incompetent doctors cause more malpractice suits, study shows

    g. Film stars die unknown and walk the earth, survey shows

    h. Brassieres cause breast cancer, study reveals. Women still wear them, research reveals.

575. If male menopause really exists, what are its symptoms? How do you know?

576. Could-be Proverbs

    a. Street sweepers dream of cottony sands.

    b. One bird cannot fly on three wings.

    c. Scars are the earth from which courage grows.

    d. All that is gold does not glitter.

    e. Happiness grows when the clock slows.

    f. Old politicians can lie in their sleep.

    g. Even whales can have small dreams.

    h. Three sheep do not make a sweater.

    i. A culture lasts only as long as its love of old people.

Select *three* could-be proverbs and explain what you think each means.

577. What myths would you change and how?

Myths

ANDREA SCHMIDT

dreams can come true

There was once a girl named Giggles who loved flowers and winter. One terrible day her mother got sick. Her father had died when she was born, so she had no uplifting man. Her mother was very sick and she could not work anymore, so she told her daughter she would someday be alone without anybody. Years passed and her mother was buried near their home so the beautiful Giggles would visit her only everybody everyday. Giggles grew old and never knew the feeling of true love with a Gorgeous man. She wished to someday tell a young girl how she herself imagined love but she knew that it would only throw the young girl off into her fantasy land.

On her Mother's sixteenth anniversary she felt as if something had suddenly changed her life. A little girl had stepped onto her garden by accident. This little girl was wishing upon a star to have a handsome prince show up at her mother's door for her mother was suffering from heartbreak. Somebody had stolen the family ring. The young Alexxia told Giggles that she had been playing with it the day it disappeared. Alexxia did not find a handsome prince at her mother's door but a poor beggar.

The mother let the man in and helped him settle into their home even though it was completely out of the town's rules. He became the man of the family. This the old Giggles had seen in the ruby ring that young princess Alexxia had given her. Giggles saw men hold the frail hands of young girls being led to the stars. She hoped to find the pretty princess out with a gorgeous man she thought decent for her.

Myths (*continued*)

Eight years later Alexxia returned to the old woman who kept the ring. She said she had a star for her. The young Alexxia was sixteen years old and married. She wished for the beautiful Giggles to be the nanny of her little princess and tell her stories of the distant universe that she had wished to tell a little girl.

OUTSIDE THE CASTLE WALLS

The ugly duckling became a beautiful swan
She flies so gracefully
Like a fairy of Elvin times
Me with my wet, dirty, stringy hair
Standing in the middle of the road
The rain pouring
The sky gray with greed
Storming at my very next step
I longed for an explanation
An explanation to my foulness
Why was I not beautiful? Why was I so perfect but not
    flowerlike?
I had no wings
I had no pearls
And I didn't want any
Why does foulness run about me?
As if to protect me from what is so glasslike
Fragile as I wish to be
I don't see the mirror
I don't see the mistake of the wings
I see the tornado that separates me from the world
I am not what I wish
I fell in love with the most beautiful place
The place that the riches call hell
The street full of poor homeless souls
I fell in love with the danger outside the castle walls
I fell in love with the ugly duckling

578. How would you define the changes in the stereotyping of nerds?

The New Aged Nerd
BRIAN FOUTS

It wasn't long ago that "nerds" were regarded with disgust and hatred, where showing even the slightest bit of intelligence in front of your peers would cause you to be given a "wedgie," tossed in a trash can, and rolled down a hill into a tree. A time where "jocks" ran the school, and smashing a beer can upon one's own forehead was considered a sign of masculinity (apparently the masculine thing to do was kill as many brain cells as possible in a short period of time). At the time, many of those intelligent people wore suspenders, a pocket protector, and could find nothing more entertaining than the previous night's episode of Star Trek. It was the stereotype of the time, but it's not to say it wasn't an accurate depiction of the way things were. But things have changed dramatically since then; nerds keep the country running, and those "jock" individuals who make a point of acting as stupid as possible, tend to turn out to be worthless leaches of society. These "nerds" have evolved since then; today, they are what I like to call "new aged nerds." A rage of emotions that is capable of brawling both physically and mentally with great precision, because they often combine the two, whereas someone else might just "go nuts" and "let whatever happens, happen." I am a new aged nerd; I am not ashamed to admit that I enjoy being able to rely on my intellect, and not my ability to invoke physical intimidation in my social predators. I don't watch Star Trek, I don't speak through my nose, I don't wear pocket protectors, and I don't really listen to musical genres outside rock and metal. I am evolved, I am strong, and I am a nerd.

---

579. At your high school, do the AS/AP classes define social groups or intellectual groups? What are the differences if any?

580. Do you judge people by the condition of their fingernails? Are they clean, too long, polished? Do you believe people of the upper class exhibit better nail care?

581. Why do your hair and nails continue to grow after you're dead?

Have you visited a funeral home and asked this question? What kinds of funerals are most expensive?

582. Does the term *light-years* measure time or space? Or both? How do you know?

583. Tanka? Why?

> *above the old cabin*
> *my habitual moon*
> *two owls still asking*
> *who? to me . . .*
> *to me?*

584. What is the difference between dry rot and wet rot?

585. American Film Titles You Won't See
   a. The Greediest President
   b. Cheerleaders Who Love Calculus
   c. A Documentary History of U.S. Peace Movements
   d. Frolicking in the Hills (a musical featuring gay teenagers)
   e. The Nazis Are Us
   f. Teens Who Turn Down Narcotics
   g. The Virtue of Innocent Women
   h. Estelle Who Didn't Wear Designer Clothes
   i. Erasmus, the Friendly Cockroach
   j. The History of Impotence in Politicians
   k. Benedict Arnold Was a Patriot . . . to the Wrong Country

   What would your *five* movie titles be?

586. Who invented the piggy bank? Why?

587. What *five* movies most definitely reveal the way you believe most women think of men? What *five* movies most clearly reveal the way most men think of women? What does each reveal?

588. If schooling is such a great idea, why is it compulsory? Jail time is mandatory. Elections are free. You can vote or not vote. What is the difference?

589. Is memorizing a good practice? What can you easily memorize? What is hard for you?

590. What are the *six* great steps to accepting growing old?

591. What is the meaning of the statement, "A girl can lose her virginity before she knows what it is"?

592. Children join gangs to feel as if they belong and are safe. Do you agree or disagree? Why?

593. Headlines focus on what is sensational. What are the most hyperbolic headlines you can imagine? Consider the following examples:
   a. President asks for homeland for visiting martians
   b. Too much sleep a national threat!
   c. American people proved loving everyone
   d. Congress votes that honesty is good
   e. Congress signs bill to allow the South to secede

594. What flavor of ice cream would you like to see invented and why?

595. Country and western music is known for its unconventional lyrics and titles. For example:
   a. He left me owing a loan and only lonely.
   b. She broke my heart without me in it.

  c. She took my saddle and left me the bridle.

  d. Now I'm riding cactus, wishing for grass.

  What *five* titles or lyrics can you write?

596. Headlines from the Asian tabloids. Write your favorite *ten*!

Zen master proven by courts zeniless

Haiku not valid defense for murder, court says

Evidence shows meditation rots your teeth

Japanese mistresses tell all—what do they really
   wear under their kimonos?

Chinese peasant sneaks into forbidden pheasant

Tokyo closing in on Bermuda Triangle

597. Why didn't Chinese women bind men's feet?

598. With modern media anyone can *seem* like anyone else. Over the phone, anyone can *seem* young, Latino, or female, and so on. On TV people can *seem* honest, important, or famous. Because the person at the other end is truly unknown, they can be what we imagine. When was the last time that you emailed someone or talked to someone on the phone, and met them in person only to find they were not at all what you imagined? How did it happen?

599. What does the word *private* mean to you? What is its connotation? How would you define privacy?

600. Why do some people believe in angels these days but not in leprechauns or trolls?

601. Make a list of *five* things that would terrify a terrorist.

602. Based on who you are today, who do you think you could have been in a former lifetime? Why?

603. What is the evolutionary reason why some kinds of camels have two humps and others have only one?

604. Who invented the steam roller for elephant pants? Why was it needed?

STUDENT SAMPLES

NOTE TO TEACHERS

I have included some of the following samples to help teachers, students, and parents learn and realize the depth of feeling in the minds of many children, known and unknown, well-known and anonymous. After many decades of teaching, I learned that most parents and teachers had little belief in the secret, harsh life of children, and were instead distanced from it, by reason of overwork, or simple unwillingness to believe, a need to feel protected; and that their children's experience was too painful to believe in. I believe these samples both realize and validate experience that might otherwise be denied. It is quite likely that the worst thing that can happen to a child is to have his own reality denied by an adult. It is my hope that the samples, both pleasurable and painful, can be believed in as real.

Silence

Jeanette Bordy

Silence can kill they say.
But, that's just what they say.
The silence of the night, the silence of the answer.
The silence of your face as
you sit there in fright.   The emotions going wild
and the look upon your face.
When I tell you I'm leaving
and there is nothing you can do.
My bags are packed, my mind is made up.
My life goes upward when the door has
been shut. I walk on steadily in good hopes and
thoughts.
There nothing you can say but "silence."

Grading Policy by Shakespeare?

POLONIUS: My lord, I will use them according to their deserts.

HAMLET: God's bodykins, man, much better: use every man after his desert, and who should 'scape whipping?

Use them after your own honour and dignity: the less they deserve, the more merit is in your bounty.

A Bottle of Whiskey

ANDREA SCHMIDT

Look at her
The boy
Soft eyes
Brown eyed
Starred suddenly
Crime Guilty
Sadly used
Struck with gold
Waiting all over
Loss of stars
Peaceful revenge
Ignored by love
Accomplished fully
Wasted and used
She sits in the sun

Made a Widow

She was made a widow 4 minutes after she was married.
On her way home she only remembered good days.
A wish under moonlight.
Her spirit dying with every step she took toward a blank
 space.
Her once red beating heart turning into a pious black hole
 swallowing her feelings.
She reached for the clouds crying for a memory.
Falling on her knees sobbing with pain and swallowing the
 choking anguish of her loss.
She saw her rose, the one they had (both) married.
She saw the memory replay with great light feeling the
 wind blow against her skin.
Her gown stained with pain and sorrow.
A new world waited for her.
Dreaming toward heaven, with her crimson skies giving
 her rest, she opened her eyes and remembered her 4
 minutes of her joyous gift.
Pain crawled on her throat.
Her tears could no longer keep their shape.
Agony no longer kept her heart for a glass coffin con-
 cealed it.

Gold

ROSE PENDLETON

Gold intertwined with lace
Removed in a form
Beyond our race

Tracing lines
Upon my page
Written words

Lost in rage
Aging speaks
On higher ground

Mountains high
Men are low
Crumbling
From dust to bone

Chasing dust
As it gathers
Deeper into
The Heart of stone

The dragon stirs
His wings expand
Exposing jewels
Of ruby and sand

Gold *continued*

His eyes
Glint bright
With stone

His teeth, his teeth, his claws, his toes
Are made from skin and bone

He hides his bulk
In folds and creases
Chasing heaven
And eats its pieces

Fire high
Like mountaintop
Skin scorched
Blood stops

The dragon rage
Pushed to leave his cage
He holds himself
In high esteem
Locked in a cage
Of my own dream

Fantasying knights
In hero's sheen
Chasing stars
Lost in dreams

O, chase my stars
With sword and song
My knight, my god

My lover
Can you but picture this
A kiss upon my sweet lips
Chase me down

Snare my soul
Capture
What was already told

I give you this
A last chance to list
All that matters, dear

Then I leave
But the dragon
Stays
To gnash and gnaw your tears

Earth will write
Stories tell
But none have known so well
That all that matters here
Is that you have won, my dear

For Related Topics on Thinking and Education

Creativity by Mihaly Csikszentmihalyi
Homo Ludens by Johan Huizinga
Creativity and Intelligence by Beckson and Ganz
The Meaning of Shakespeare by Harold C. Goddard (especially
        Henry IV, Falstaff, Henry V, Much Ado About Nothing,
        Troilus and Cressida)
Standardized Minds by Peter Sacks
In Schools We Trust by Deborah Meier
One Size Fits Few by Susan Ohanian
The Schools Our Children Deserve by Aflie Kohn
Braindroppings by George Carlin
Should We Burn Babar by Herbert Kohl
Zen Haiku and Other Zen Poems by James W. Hackett
Growing Up Absurd by Paul Goodman
Light Verse from the Floating World by Makoto Ueda (senryu)
Haiku by R. H. Blyth (four volumes)
Senryu by R. H. Blyth
Fooling with Words by Bill Moyers
The Prentice-Hall Encyclopedia of World Proverbs by Wolfgang
        Mieder

Afterword

This book is intended to move from the ridiculous to the sublime. I have organized it by the disarray found in nature that allows us to pick and choose what we wish to see as beautiful, just as we do in a child or woman or man who, for no reason at all, we remember years later by the manner in which she poured us tea, or the way he swatted flies. The way our favorite grandmother brushed her white hair on the porch in the moonlight. Teaching writing, as many young and old teachers do in the five paragraph form, from the outside in, is like making a snail's shell first and then bidding him to live and love there.

There are many other procrustean writing forms that are unfortunate mistakes in that they don't allow room for growth. Nor discovery of their own voice. They keep growth contained within to the point that, like skin, the spirit or personality leaves the same stretch marks that every nursing mother knows. Adolescents, both mind and body, are growing spirits, and I would not wish to see them dammed up where the stones end, prepared for a life built by snail shells with nothing in them.

Forms, when they have been learned and not forgotten deep down, teach obedience while imagination teaches freedom. Not freedom from all forms or forms at all, but the freedom to use them or not use them at will. Standardized tests fashion standardized minds. I doubt if the motive for such tests is to harm. But the result is the same. In our culture shaped after the metaphor of mass production, we value team players, people who are on the same page, people who can get their ducks in a row, and a thousand others. In other words, conformists. Quality assurance means that every product is like every other one in quality. No differences. Without differences, no individuality. The Maker has become anonymous. And yet in human affairs, we love a friend who has a pebble from the stream that holds a turquoise vein, or an antique shell that still holds the ocean's roar.

And, were I to love my patient wife and three spiritual sons with such lack of imagination, with anonymity, without such love of differences, I would have been absent of age-old beauty long ago. I would have been the snail's shell.

And in the world of these wandering prompts, I hope each Maker does not become anonymous. Each child who waits on a desk in a classroom awaits something that makes his individual differences make sense. I do not think they wait to be a future conformist. I think they await being awakened from their daily, routine mind into some world where their imagination and its ideas long to go down the ancient paths of humanity.

Our children and students climb either on the earth or on a star. I prefer a star! There are paths that lead that way.